Awesome Asian Animals

A+
books

Giant
Pandas
Are
Awesome

by Megan Cooley Peterson

Consultant: Jackie Gai, DVM
Wildlife Veterinarian
Vacaville, California

CAPSTONE PRESS
a capstone imprint

A+ Books are published by Capstone Press,
1710 Roe Crest Drive, North Mankato, Minnesota 56003
www.capstonepub.com

Library of Congress Cataloging-in-Publication Data
Peterson, Megan Cooley, author.
Giant pandas are awesome! / by Megan Cooley Peterson.
pages cm. — (A+ books. Awesome Asian animals)
Summary: "Introduces young readers to giant pandas, including physical characteristics, behavior, habitat, diet,
and life cycle"— Provided by publisher.
Audience: Ages 4–8.
Audience: K to grade 3.
Includes bibliographical references and index.
ISBN 978-1-4914-3905-0 (library binding)
ISBN 978-1-4914-3924-1 (paperback)
ISBN 978-1-4914-3934-0 (eBook PDF)
1. Giant panda—Juvenile literature. I. Title.
QL737.C27P4256 2016
599.789—dc23   2014045058

Editorial Credits
Michelle Hasselius, editor; Peggie Carley, designer; Tracy Cummins, media researcher;
Morgan Walters, production specialist

Photo Credits
Capstone Press: 16; Getty Images: Glowimages, 18 Bottom, Joe Petersburger, 14 Top, Keren Su, 18 Top;
iStockphoto: mchen007, 21 Top, 22 L, mrbfaust, 14 Bottom, Rchang, 11, samkee, 4, yesfoto, 10; Minden Pictures:
Cyril Ruoso, 20, 21 Bottom, Katherine Feng, 13 Bottom, 24, 25, Konrad Wothe, 17, Thomas Marent, 12 Bottom,
Tony Heald/npl, 28; Shutterstock: Eric Isselee, Cover L, Cover Top R, Cover Back, 1, 26 Left, 30, 32, Hung
Chung Chih, Cover Bottom, 6, 8, 19, 22 R, 26 R, 29 Top, leungchopan, 9, lzf, 29 Bottom, nattanan726, 12 Top,
15, Rigamondis, Design Element, Sergey Dzyuba, 7, silverjohn, 23, 27, TonyV3112, 5.

Note to Parents, Teachers, and Librarians
This Awesome Asian Animals book uses full color photographs and a nonfiction format to introduce
the concept of giant pandas. *Giant Pandas Are Awesome!* is designed to be read aloud to a pre-reader or
to be read independently by an early reader. Photographs help listeners and early readers understand
the text and concepts discussed. The book encourages further learning by including the following
sections: Table of Contents, Glossary, Read More, Internet Sites, Critical Thinking Using the Common
Core, and Index. Early readers may need assistance using these features.

Printed in the United States   5002

Table of Contents

Bonkers for Bamboo

A giant panda yanks down a bamboo stem. The panda sits on its hind legs and holds the bamboo with its front paws. The panda plucks leaves from the bamboo. Then it grinds the leaves and stem with its teeth.

Giant pandas spend about 14 hours a day munching on bamboo. Adult pandas eat 20 to 40 pounds (9 to 18 kilograms) of bamboo a day. These mammals' stomachs can't break down plants very well. To get enough nutrients, pandas eat a lot of bamboo.

A Giant Panda's Body

What's black and white and furry all over? A giant panda! Giant pandas have white heads with black eye patches and black ears. They also have black arms and legs. White fur covers short tails.

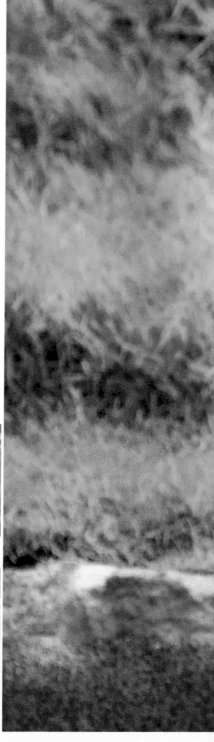

Giant pandas belong to the bear family. Adult pandas weigh up to 250 pounds (113 kg). They stand up to 3 feet (0.9 meter) tall at the shoulders.

Giant pandas have small, dark eyes that see well. Unlike most bears, pandas do not have round pupils. They have narrow, catlike pupils. In China the giant panda is called a bear cat.

A giant panda uses its sense of smell to help it in the wild. Pandas use their noses to find food and other pandas. Young pandas use their noses to sniff out dangerous animals, such as the golden cat and yellow-throated marten. But adult pandas have few predators.

Giant pandas have five
strong claws on each paw. They
also have a long wrist bone in
each front paw. The bones help
pandas grasp bamboo.

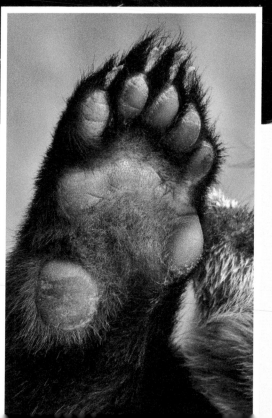

Open wide! A giant panda has strong jaws and 42 teeth for eating bamboo. Sharp front teeth slice the tough plant. Its wide, flat back teeth crush and chew.

Life in the Mountains

All wild giant pandas live in the bamboo forests of central China. Pandas prefer cool, wet forests high in the mountains.

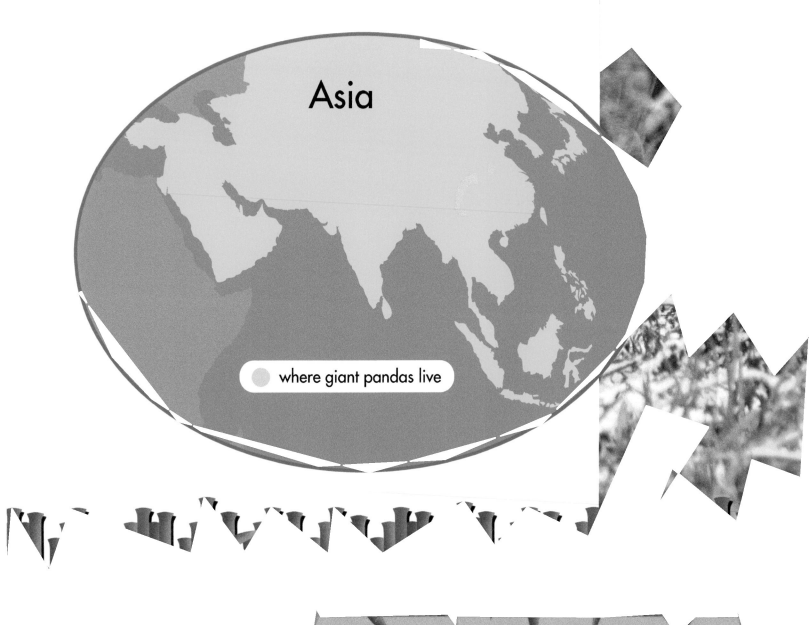

Asia

⬤ where giant pandas live

Giant pandas do not hibernate like other bears. In colder months they move to lower areas of the mountains, where it's warmer.

Giant pandas live alone, except when mothers raise their cubs. Adults have their own home ranges. A panda uses its scent to communicate with other giant pandas. Pandas rub their bodies against trees. They scrape trees and the ground with their claws. Their scents let other pandas know where they've been.

Giant pandas don't roar like other bears. But they do make lots of sounds. Pandas huff and snort when upset. They bleat like lambs to say hello. Females bark at males when it's time to mate.

Giant pandas communicate with their bodies. They lower their heads and stare at other pandas to scare them away. Pandas cover their eye patches with their paws when they're afraid. When it's playtime, pandas roll around on the ground.

Giant pandas spend most of their days looking for and eating bamboo. Bamboo gives pandas most of the water they need. But they also drink water from rivers and streams. To save energy, pandas don't travel very far each day.

Giant pandas curl up under trees to sleep.
Sometimes they snooze up high in trees.
Pandas sleep from two to six hours at a time.

Growing Up Giant Panda

Female giant pandas give birth to one or two cubs in fall. Cubs weigh about 5 ounces (142 grams) at birth. They are 7 inches (18 centimeters) long. That's about as long as a tube of toothpaste!

Newborn panda cubs can't see or hear. They have pink skin and little fur. Cubs stay warm by snuggling with their mothers. By winter cubs grow a full coat of fur.

Giant panda cubs love to play. They climb on their mothers and swat at them. Mothers nuzzle their cubs. They also teach their cubs how to find and eat bamboo. Cubs stay with their mothers for about three years. Giant pandas live about 20 years in the wild.

Saving Giant Pandas

When bamboo forests are cut down, pandas don't have enough food to eat. Roads and towns make it hard for pandas to move to new forests. Because of this giant pandas are endangered. Fewer than 2,500 pandas live in the wild.

Today zoos breed giant pandas. In the wild, land is set aside for pandas to live on. People want to save these awesome Asian animals.

Glossary

breed (BREED)—to mate and produce young

cub (KUHB)—a young animal such as a panda, cheetah, lion, or tiger

endangered (in-DAYN-juhrd)—in danger of dying out

hibernate (HYE-bur-nate)—to spend winter in a deep sleep

mammal (MAM-uhl)—a warm–blooded animal that breathes air; mammals have hair or fur

mate (MATE)—to join together to produce young

nutrient (NOO-tree-uhnt)—a substance living things need to stay healthy

predator (PRED-uh-tur)—an animal that hunts another animal for food

pupil (PYOO-puhl)—the dark center of the eye that lets in light

range (RAYNJ)—an area where an animal mostly lives

Read More

Brett, Jeannie. *Wild About Bears.* Watertown, Mass.: Charlesbridge, 2014.

Kolpin, Molly. *Giant Pandas.* Bears. Mankato, Minn.: Capstone Press, 2012.

Royston, Angela. *Save the Giant Panda.* Animal SOS! New York: Windmill Books, 2014.

Internet Sites

FactHound offers a safe, fun way to find Internet sites related to this book. All of the sites on FactHound have been researched by our staff.

Here's all you do:
Visit *www.facthound.com*
Type in this code: 9781491439050

Check out projects, games and lots more at
www.capstonekids.com

Critical Thinking Using the Common Core

1. Giant pandas have their own ranges. What is a range? (Craft and Structure)

2. Giant pandas use their bodies to communicate with other pandas. How does a panda tell others it is scared? (Key Ideas and Details)

3. Giant pandas are endangered. What are people doing to try to save the giant panda? (Key Ideas and Details)

Index

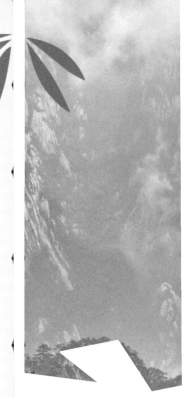